BEATING BURNOUT:

*A 30-Day Guide to
Hope and Health*

Anne Marie Miller

Beating Burnout: A 30-Day Guide to Hope and Health

Copyright © 2014 by Anne Marie Miller

Requests for information should be addressed to:

Anne Marie Miller, anne@annemariemiller.com

Miller, Anne Marie 1980 –

Beating burnout: A 30-day guide to hope and health /

Anne Marie Miller

ISBN-10: 0991373510

ISBN-13: 978-0-9913735-1-2

1. Burn out (Psychology) — Religious aspects, Christianity;

2. Devotional literature, English

Devotionals 8, 19, 25 & 26 are excerpted from Mad Church Disease: Healing from Church Burnout and 15 and 21 are excerpted from Lean on Me: Finding Intentional, Vulnerable and Consistent Community, both © Anne Marie Miller.

Interior design by Holy City Design

··

Author's Note:

Knowing that all health stems from our Creator, for the sake of practical application and study, this devotional is structured using six themes: rest, spiritual health, emotional health, relational health, physical health, and prayer.

Though each devotional piece builds on those before it and is intended to be a daily devotional, please use it however you need to. There is no right or wrong way to study God's Word and meditate on His truth. We are multifaceted and dynamic beings, so many of these themes overlap. What is physical is also spiritual, what is relational is also emotional, and so on.

Please use the space provided to record your thoughts and prayers as you spend some extra time with your Father who loves you so dearly.

Should you have any questions or prayer requests as you move through these daily meditations, do not hesitate to contact me at anne@annemariemiller.com. I would love to hear from you and learn about your journey.

The grace of our Lord Jesus Christ be with your spirit,
Anne Marie Miller

··

TABLE OF CONTENTS

Day 1 – Rest: Set Apart   2

Day 2 – Spiritual Health: Secret Sin   4

Day 3 – Relational Health: Confession   6

Day 4 – Emotional Health: Emotional Abundance   8

Day 5 – Physical Health: Defining Healthy Habits   10

Day 6 – Prayer   12

Day 7 – Rest: A Quiet Trust   14

Day 8 – Spiritual Health: Meditating on God's Word   16

Day 9 – Relational Health: Being Peacemakers   18

Day 10 – Emotional Health: Anxiety   20

Day 11 – Physical Health: Healthy Eating   22

Day 12 – Prayer   24

Day 13 – Rest: Shelter   26

Day 14 – Spiritual Health: Protect Yourself   28

Day 15 – Relational Health: Needing Others Appropriately   30

Day 16 – Emotional Health: Pride   32

Day 17 – Physical Health: Exercise   34

Day 18 – Prayer   36

Day 19 – Rest: Resting with Jesus   38

Day 20 – Spiritual Health: Trusting God   40

Day 21 – Relational Health: Are You Needy?   42

Day 22 – Emotional Health: Discouragement & Depression   44

Day 23 – Physical Health: Sleeping Habits   46

Day 24 – Prayer   48

Day 25 – Rest: Holy Sacrifices   50

Day 26 – Spiritual Health: An Abundant Life   52

Day 27 – Relational Health: The Need to Belong   54

Day 28 – Emotional Health: Anger & Apathy   56

Day 29 – Physical Health: It's Not Just Physical   58

Day 30 – Prayer   60

DAY 1

Scripture:
"On the seventh day God had finished his work of creation, so he rested from all his work. And God blessed the seventh day and declared it holy, because it was the day when he rested from all his work of creation" (Genesis 2:2–3).

One of the very first mentions of rest in the Bible happens immediately after God creates everything. His work was finished and He rested.

Not only did He rest, He "blessed the seventh day and declared it holy." He set apart this day of rest from the days He worked and created.

God is infinite in power and strength. He needs nothing and lacks nothing, yet He rested. Perhaps in His knowledge, He knew mankind would need rest and this was an eternal example for us to follow.

Reflect:
We work, we create, we tarry, we worry. We are finite in all we are and all we do. If God Himself set a day aside to rest, should we not follow in His example? Choose to embrace a day of rest each week—a day that is sacred in ways that are beyond our comprehension. When we rest, we step aside and allow our God to do His work through us and prepare us for the work He has for us to do.

My day of rest this week will be:

notes

DAY 2

Scripture:
"People judge by outward appearance, but the Lord looks at the heart" (1 Samuel 16:7b).

One way we burn out is by carrying unnecessary spiritual weight. We see in 1 Samuel that people on the outside can judge us on what they see, but God looks at our hearts.

I remember when I first started getting sick in my own season of burn-out. You could look at me and think my whole life was a well-oiled machine. I looked nice, I acted nice, I was never late for a deadline, I could pray for others and knew my Bible back and forth. But inside? My soul was dying.

God knew my heart, and He knew my pride, my greed, my envy . . . all of my secret sins. I was buried under the burden of the weight of them.

Reflect:
One of the first steps we must take to become healthy is to set our secrets free. Keep in mind this saying: "We're only as sick as our secrets." By confessing our hidden sin to God and to others, we'll discover the first step toward finding freedom and spiritual health.

What are the sins you carry inside? Who can you confess them to this week?

notes

DAY 3

Scripture:
"Share each other's burdens, and in this way obey the law of Christ. If you think you are too important to help someone, you are only fooling yourself. You are not that important" (Galatians 6:2–3).

This scripture from Paul is a fairly direct statement, especially the last bit! Moving from confessing our sin to God to taking the next step of confessing our sin to others can be one of the most difficult steps, especially if we're in ministry or in a church community.

Sometimes it seems like sharing our mistakes or questions with the church is the least safe thing to do. What if we get judged? Condemned? Ostracized? If we work at a church, what if we lost our jobs and our health insurance?

The biblical response is to first understand our need to confess to others (James 5:16), and to create safe places for others to confess, too.

Reflect:
We must realize that a church or a ministry is not our provision, even if it provides our paycheck. God is our provision. The church should support people walking through repentance and restoration. When our pride gets in the way, we feel like we're "too important" to help someone. Or maybe we think others are too important to help us.

Who can you ask to help carry you as you work out your salvation? Who can you help as someone grows in their faith?

notes

DAY 4

Scripture:
"In view of all this, make every effort to respond to God's promises. Supplement your faith with a generous provision of moral excellence, and moral excellence with knowledge, and knowledge with self-control, and self-control with patient endurance, and patient endurance with godliness, and godliness with brotherly affection, and brotherly affection with love for everyone. The more you grow like this, the more productive and useful you will be in your knowledge of our Lord Jesus Christ" (2 Peter 1:5–8).

In verses 1–4 of 2 Peter 1, the author writes that we have been given everything we need in order to fulfill God's promises in our lives. We share in God's divine nature, and we're able to overcome natural desires and the world's corruption because of this.

So, in verses 5–8, we're challenged to confidently add to our faith moral excellence, self-control, patience, endurance, godliness, affection, and love. Generally speaking, these attributes are not easy to come by in the church.

When we do grow in these characteristics, we're told that we will be more productive and useful in our knowledge of Christ and the things we should set out to do as the Kingdom on earth.

Reflect:
Which of the characteristics listed in 2 Peter 1:5–8 are most difficult for you to work through? Sometimes it's easier to think we can do better on our own, but when we see that we share in God's divine nature, when our spirits are open to His leading, these attributes are natural results. Choose one or two characteristics of 2 Peter 1:5–8. Instead of "working on being better at them" as we tend to do, instead, in your prayers, ask God to help you see that these qualities are readily available to you and ask Him to give you opportunities to see Him at work in your life in these specific areas.

notes

DAY 5

Scripture:
"Dear friend, I hope all is well with you and that you are as healthy in body as you are strong in spirit" (3 John 1:2).

The author of 3 John 1:2 assumes that the person receiving the letter is strong in spirit, but may not be as healthy in body. This is just one of many references to being physically healthy in the Scriptures. In an overworked society, our physical health often suffers the most after our spiritual health.

In my first two years of ministry, I gained forty pounds. On my small 5'6" frame, that was a lot. New symptoms of my obesity crept in slowly: acid reflux, back problems, and headaches. It was easier to go through the drive-through than to make something healthy for lunch. Plus, there's something about food that's bad for us that tastes so good and can even provide comfort.

Reflect:
Eating right, sleeping, and exercising are probably the three most important basic actions we can implement into our daily routine. When even one of these is out of balance, our whole body suffers in many ways.

Share which of these three habits is the most difficult for you to maintain with a friend this week.

notes

DAY 6

Prayer days in this devotional (every sixth day) are designed to help you listen to and converse with God on anything (a scripture, an issue at hand, a praise). Maybe use the prayer section every day to supplement your daily prayers. The following structure is created to help you navigate and focus. If it doesn't fit your needs specifically, simply modify it as you need to. This isn't about getting it right; it's about communing with your Abba, Father.

• Choose a scripture that is familiar to you or that has spoken to you recently. If none comes to mind, consider one in this devotional or ask God to guide you one.

• While resting in a quiet place with no distractions, read and recite this scripture out loud several times, paying special attention to each and every word.

• Take a few moments to quiet your heart and mind. Simply sit in the presence of God, listening. If you don't hear anything or if your mind wanders, it's okay. If you don't "feel" anything, that doesn't mean God isn't saying anything. Just try to bring your attention back and focus on the idea or Bible verse at hand.

• After some time listening and sitting before God, make a list, mentally or maybe written, of things you are thankful for this week. Share them with Him and praise Him for the work He's doing.

• Confess any sins to Him, asking Him to reveal areas in your life where you can rely more fully on Him.

• Write down anything, no matter how seemingly small, that comes to mind after you spend time with Him today.

notes

DAY 7

Scripture:
"This is what the Sovereign Lord, the Holy One of Israel, says: 'Only in returning to me and resting in me will you be saved. In quietness and trust is your strength, but you would have none of it" (Isaiah 30:15).

The nation of Judah was rebelling against God and not listening to His warning. He promised them salvation if they returned and rested in Him, assuring them that His strength was perfect for them. Yet they refused and instead trusted neighboring Egypt for their help.

Ruth Haley Barton in *Leading in Rhythm* says, "As disciplines of rest, solitude, and silence rescue us from the brink of dangerous levels of exhaustion, we are restored to a state of quiet alertness, ready to receive guidance from God about what we are to do in the world."

Reflect:
The Egyptians gave Judah horses to help them in battle – something they could see and touch. Often, returning to and resting in God requires us to have faith without tangible reminders of His presence. Countless times in scripture we are told that it is only through Him that we can live abundantly and in His peace, whether we can see His gifts to us or not.

What things in your life are difficult to surrender to "resting in God?" Like Judah taking the Egyptians' horses, what are a few things that you find security in? What can you surrender and trust to God and believe that He will accomplish even as you rest?

notes

DAY 8

Scripture:
"Study this Book of Instruction continually. Meditate on it day and night so you will be sure to obey everything written in it. Only then will you prosper and succeed in all you do" (Joshua 1:8).

Studying scripture is fundamental to our spiritual health. The Bible is God's Word and His instructions to us. The Holy Spirit illuminates scripture for us. In scripture, we are taught about God's character and reminded of God's faithfulness in the past. We are instructed on how to live holy lives of love, and we are convicted of our shortcomings.

I have personally struggled with consistent Bible study. My life seems to get too busy, and I honestly sometimes just blow it off because I'm running around "doing things for God." And during the seasons when I am lazy and neglect time in God's Word, I realize how simple it is to justify sin in my life. I lose focus on truth.

During the times when we faithfully meditate on God's Word, it's amazing how scripture overflows from our minds and is applied constantly throughout our day.

Reflect:
We're always meditating on something, whether it is scripture, a blog, or a conversation we're mulling over. The key is to shift our focus to scripture and truth as we go about our day. Try keeping God's Word on your mind for a day and watch how your perspective changes.

What are three scriptures you can meditate on today, or this week? What do you expect God to do when you turn your focus to Him during your day?

notes

DAY 9

Scripture:
"God blesses those who work for peace, for they will be called the children of God" (Matthew 5:9).

Stress and burnout can cause us to project our pain and exhaustion on others — usually those closest to us. Some people respond to burnout by lashing out in anger and storming around in a rage as their lives are falling apart.

Exhaustion can cause us to shut down and stop communicating with our spouse or our friends. And by "communicating," I mean both talking and listening. We no longer feel connected to those around us, and we begin not to care about nurturing those relationships that God has placed in our lives.

After not communicating for a while, resentment can develop. Our spouses or friends may not feel comfortable opening up to us anymore, and bitterness can be formed and directed toward us, toward the church, and even toward God.

Reflect:
In Matthew 5:9, Jesus directs us to be "peacemakers." It will take effort and intentionality on our part to bring balance back into our relationships. We are to make peace and strive for unity.

Have you cut off communication with people because you're feeling burned out? Write down their names and a trait you admire about each one of them. Then write down a date you will contact them, making amends if necessary.

notes

DAY 10

Scripture:
"Give all your worries and cares to God, for he cares about you" (1 Peter 5:7).

In 1 Peter 5:7, many translations use the word "anxieties" instead of "worries or cares." Some translations even talk about "throwing" them to God. Regardless of the translation, the message to trust God with our difficulties is clear.

We all experience worry and anxiety. In some cases, we may feel overwhelmed or deeply concerned about a situation. Other times, we may have a chemical imbalance that causes our mind, body, and spirit to react with a type of anxiety that doesn't ever seem to end.

Anxiety (the chemical imbalance type) is something I've battled since I was fourteen years old. For no reason whatsoever, one evening as I did homework, I was overcome with fear and panic. My body physically responded to the anxiety. Now, twenty years later, I manage the symptoms through a holistic approach: my time with God, support from friends, treating my body kindly, counseling, and many times, with medication.

Mental illness, including anxiety, isn't often spoken about in faith environments. I can't tell you how many times I've been told, "You don't have enough faith. God will heal you from this!" or "You must have some sort of sin in your life. Isn't worry a sin?" But in His plan, He has not chosen to release me from anxiety.

Reflect:
Even though anxiety is a daily burden, God has shown me ways to rely on Him and others. When I lean into Him, although it may still be a struggle, it doesn't hinder me from living in the abundance He has for me. It doesn't have to hold you back either.

What things cause you to worry or have anxiety? Have you shared this with others? In what ways can you treat the anxieties that come your way?

notes

DAY 11

Scripture:
"The earth is the Lord's and all its fullness" (Psalm 24:1, NKJV).

Let's start this quest toward physical health by eating healthy and concentrating on the things we put in our bodies.

I understand that there are many philosophies on what people believe is good to eat. Some think everything is permissible, but in keeping with Paul's teaching, not everything is beneficial. Some believe eating vegan or vegetarian is humane, others like a big steak and eggs meal.

Regardless of what you personally believe, there is a healthy way to eat. A few of the things I think about when I get food, whether through the grocer, out at a restaurant, or when making it myself, include:

1) *Is this going to contribute to my overall well being? (Is it healthy? Will it nourish me?)*
2) *Will this choice make someone near me struggle? (Am I consuming something that another person can't because of a personal decision like sobriety, lifestyle choices, or allergies?)*
3) *Is this a good use of the money God's given me?*
4) *Am I eating this or drinking this in order to be comforted or escape from an emotion?*

In the last few years, I've developed allergies to wheat (gluten) and dairy. Because of this, my husband Tim and I eat produce-rich, healthy grains (quinoa, brown rice), and lean meats (fish, local chicken, turkey). We also use plant proteins and fruit for smoothies. We drink a lot of water, and rarely will have sweets, fast food, soda, or alcohol.

Even if you don't have the same allergies I have, I can tell you that these lifestyle changes have made a significant difference in both of our moods, sleeping patterns, energy, and health. If the allergies magically disappeared one day, we'd continue eating this way.

Reflect:

Keep a food journal for a week or use an app like "Lose It" to keep a record of what you eat. Count things like calories, fats, carbohydrates, sugars, fiber, and protein, and note when you eat them. It's easy to find an online tool and see what the recommended daily value is for your height, weight, and age.

After keeping track for a week, do you notice any trends? Are there areas when you can make healthier decisions about the food and beverages you consume?

notes

_____

_____

_____

_____

_____

_____

_____

_____

_____

_____

_____

_____

_____

_____

DAY 12

Prayer days in this devotional (every sixth day) are designed to help you listen to and converse with God on anything (a scripture, an issue at hand, a praise). Maybe use the prayer section every day to supplement your daily prayers. The following structure is created to help you navigate and focus. If it doesn't fit your needs specifically, simply modify it as you need to. This isn't about getting it right; it's about communing with your Abba, Father.

• Choose a scripture that is familiar to you or that has spoken to you recently. If none comes to mind, consider one in this devotional or ask God to guide you one.

• While resting in a quiet place with no distractions, read and recite this scripture out loud several times, paying special attention to each and every word.

• Take a few moments to quiet your heart and mind. Simply sit in the presence of God, listening. If you don't hear anything or if your mind wanders, it's okay. If you don't "feel" anything, that doesn't mean God isn't saying anything. Just try to bring your attention back and focus on the idea or Bible verse at hand.

• After some time listening and sitting before God, make a list, mentally or maybe written, of things you are thankful for this week. Share them with Him and praise Him for the work He's doing.

• Confess any sins to Him, asking Him to reveal areas in your life where you can rely more fully on Him.

• Write down anything, no matter how seemingly small, that comes to mind after you spend time with Him today.

notes

DAY 13

Scripture:
"Those who live in the shelter of the Most High will find rest in the shadow of the Almighty" (Psalm 91:1).

I grew up in Tornado Alley. At a very early age, I was taught to head to the tornado shelter if the sirens went off in the small farm town where I lived.

It was something I had to do on a fairly regular basis. The sirens would go off, and down into the shelter I went with my family or classmates. Once we were underground, I didn't worry. Sure, there were times I wondered if my house got blown away, but any real fear disappeared. I trusted the shelter to keep me safe.

Similarly, we can live in the shelter God gives us. We can find rest and peace when we focus on the greatness of our Savior. The words in Psalm 91, "rest in the shadow of the Almighty," show us two things: our God is big, and He is a source of light.

Reflect:
When life feels like a storm, meditate on this verse. Think of yourself as a small child being wrapped into a blanket where you're totally safe and totally protected. There is nothing you can do when a tornado hits; it's out of your control. There's also often nothing you can do when the storms of life hit. Rest in His shelter.

Write out Psalm 91:1 in your own words and put it in a place you'll see it frequently. The next time you're feeling swept up and you can't rest, repeat it as you take deep breaths, focusing on the truth that you can rest in God.

notes

DAY 14

Scripture:
"A final word: Be strong in the Lord and in his mighty power. Put on all of God's armor so that you will be able to stand firm against all strategies of the devil. For we are not fighting against flesh-and-blood enemies, but against evil rulers and authorities of the unseen world, against mighty powers in this dark world, and against evil spirits in the heavenly places" *(Ephesians 6:10–12).*

Submission is the enemy of our human will and the opposite of every-thing our hearts desire. We crave our rights. We demand our freedom.

Not our will, Lord, but yours be done. That should be our prayer. The tension between pursuing our own desires, hopes, and dreams and pursuing what God has for us can cause such confusion and distraction.

This is where Satan loves to get us every time.

It's an uphill spiritual battle to live the abundant life God has called us to. John tells us in John 10:10 that the enemy's sole purpose — his only intent — is to destroy us. However, by equipping ourselves with the armor of God and by submitting to Him (relying on His protection and His power), we are promised that the devil will flee. And we are promised life to the fullest.

Reflect:
Have you ever said, "I just can't take this anymore!" and wanted to give up? Then, if you gave up, did you feel defeated and find it was difficult to move forward with something else? The enemy loves to lure us into this cycle. Scripture says the same power that raised Christ from the dead lives in us. We can take this power, and in those moments we need to fight (often for our own spiritual rest), know we have heavenly armies fighting on our side.

notes

DAY 15

Scripture:

"Jesus called his twelve disciples together and gave them authority to cast out evil spirits and to heal every kind of disease and illness. Here are the names of the twelve apostles: first, Simon (also called Peter), then Andrew (Peter's brother), James (son of Zebedee), John (James's brother), Philip, Bartholomew, Thomas, Matthew (the tax collector), James (son of Alphaeus), Thaddaeus, Simon (the zealot), Judas Iscariot (who later betrayed him)" (Matthew 10:1-4).

When looking at the men Jesus surrounded himself with—His closest community, the disciples—I see the diversity in those He chose.

Peter was impulsive, but out of all the other disciples, was the only one who had faith to take a step onto the sea to walk on water. Matthew was a tax collector who liked making enemies. Simon—the zealot—was passionate and often appeared to have a bit of an angry personality. Thomas was likely on the other end of the spectrum. He doubted and required proof of Jesus' scars so he could believe it was truly his Lord who had risen from the dead.

However, the disciples' personalities described to us in Scripture don't stay consistent during Jesus' ministry. Impulsive Peter is later called "The Rock." Thomas' doubt turned into belief. As they walked with this grace-filled, divine man, their lives were transformed. They began taking on characteristics of the Rabbi they followed.

Reflect:

When close relationships are diverse, not only do you have the chance to learn from other perspectives, by default, you begin acquiring the qualities of those you spend time with. What are some characteristics you'd like to see improved in your life?

notes

DAY 16

Scripture:
"Pride leads to disgrace, but with humility comes wisdom" (Proverbs 11:2).

Living like Christ can seem like a paradox at times. We're supposed to be leaders and servants at the same time. In our current culture, leaders are generally seen as having charismatic personalities that attract followers. Leaders are the ones who get book deals, who have big churches, or who are in charge of large organizations. They are the super moms and dads who manage perfect households. We see them as the perfect Christians.

While this may be one perception of what a leader looks like, Jesus challenges us that whoever is the greatest is really the smallest. The one who leads the most is the one who serves the most. Living in this tension is difficult, especially in the "church world" where we get accolades for the big things we do.

When I look at the other great things people do, it's easy for me to get jealous or bitter and want the attention they get. Or, whenever I have something go well for me, I pat myself on the back and get a big head.

Proverbs tells us pride leads to disgrace, but wisdom comes with humility. When we're tied up in what others are doing, our disgrace may not be public, but it can lead to us feeling emotionally depleted or discouraged.

Reflect:
On an emotional level, neither envy or pride are good reactions. We have to constantly seek out humility. We need to be people who are always ready to serve anyone, anytime, anywhere.

Are there certain situations where you find yourself feeling prideful, either by being jealous or thinking too much of yourself? Which do you struggle the most with? Does it discourage you?

notes

DAY 17

Scripture:
"Don't you realize that in a race everyone runs, but only one person gets the prize? So run to win! All athletes are disciplines in their training. They do it to win a prize that will fade away, but we do it for an eternal prize. So I run with purpose in every step. I am not just shadowboxing. I discipline my body like an athlete, training it to do what it should. Otherwise, I fear that after my preaching to others I myself might be disqualified" (1 Corinthians 9:24-27).

This verse in 1 Corinthians is a familiar one that is often used to talk about exercise. Paul wrote this passage in this way because his audience was familiar with keeping in good physical shape. He drew the parallel of physical discipline to spiritual discipline.

Yet, the physical discipline he writes about shouldn't be dismissed as only metaphor. Even Paul kept his body in peak shape so that his witness would never be called into question spiritually.

The discipline of exercise is just that: a discipline. A minority of the world's population actually enjoys it. Fewer find time for it. Since working full time, I've fallen out of my exercise discipline many, many times —and being an "all or nothing" kind of person, it's easy to get discouraged when I have to begin again.

There are so many benefits of exercising: physical health (cardio health, muscle and bone health); emotional health (the release of "good" hormones and chemicals); relational health (joining a gym or group); and spiritual health (listening to music, praying or meditating as you exercise). Although exercise may help you lose weight if you need to, it's not just about the scale. It's about maintaining discipline and health.

Reflect:
If you don't exercise, set a goal to simply get moving. Go for a 30-minute walk (or break it into 10 minute segments if 30 minutes at one time is hard to do). Try a new class with friends or join a gym. You can even exercise in the privacy of your own home through Netflix or DVDs. There are many online groups you can join as well.

notes

DAY 18

Prayer days in this devotional (every sixth day) are designed to help you listen to and converse with God on anything (a scripture, an issue at hand, a praise). Maybe use the prayer section every day to supplement your daily prayers. The following structure is created to help you navigate and focus. If it doesn't fit your needs specifically, simply modify it as you need to. This isn't about getting it right; it's about communing with your Abba, Father.

• Choose a scripture that is familiar to you or that has spoken to you recently. If none comes to mind, consider one in this devotional or ask God to guide you one.

• While resting in a quiet place with no distractions, read and recite this scripture out loud several times, paying special attention to each and every word.

• Take a few moments to quiet your heart and mind. Simply sit in the presence of God, listening. If you don't hear anything or if your mind wanders, it's okay. If you don't "feel" anything, that doesn't mean God isn't saying anything. Just try to bring your attention back and focus on the idea or Bible verse at hand.

• After some time listening and sitting before God, make a list, mentally or maybe written, of things you are thankful for this week. Share them with Him and praise Him for the work He's doing.

• Confess any sins to Him, asking Him to reveal areas in your life where you can rely more fully on Him.

• Write down anything, no matter how seemingly small, that comes to mind after you spend time with Him today.

notes

DAY 19

Scripture:
"Then Jesus said, "Let's go off by ourselves to a quiet place and rest awhile."
He said this because there were so many people coming and going that
Jesus and his apostles didn't even have time to eat" (Mark 6:31).

In Mark 6, Jesus sends the apostles out two by two to do His work. It was one of those "all hands on deck" kind of seasons. They were incredibly busy, incredibly hurried. And even as they filed their report with Jesus, there was such a hustle and bustle of activity around them that they didn't have a chance to eat.

Busy? Hurried? Skipping meals?

Yep. Sounds like ministry.

And they pushed through.

After spending some time with Jesus, instead of heading straight back into their ministry, they are commanded to rest.

"Let's go off by ourselves to a quiet place and rest awhile."

Jesus knew that the apostles needed to rest. Alone. But also with Him.

Reflect:
Jesus is telling you to come to Him to find rest. You don't need a burning bush. He tells you through Scripture. He tells you through circumstances and people. He speaks this invitation to you when your soul is empty and your heart can't take any more.

How do you hear God telling you to rest?

notes

DAY 20

Scripture:
"They [the righteous] do not fear bad news; they confidently trust the Lord to care for them" (Psalm 112:7).

After being betrayed by someone I served with at a church, I found it incredibly difficult to trust. This seemingly private issue had a big impact on my relationship with God and with others. I was certainly not living an abundant life.

Satan will do anything to beat us down and make us ineffective for the Kingdom. This includes warping our perspective on trusting God, others, and ourselves again.

One of the first steps in learning to trust again is realizing that unless we fully trust God and His sovereignty, it will be impossible to trust others. But we must remain steadfast in our pursuit of trust.

When someone betrays your trust, it crushes your heart. The Hebrew word translated "steadfast" is kûn, which means "to be erect, to set up — confirm, direct, faithfulness, be fixed, be stable."

We are promised that when we trust the Lord, our hearts become capable of being fixed and stable — even in those times when we face difficult circumstances.

Reflect:
Is it hard for you to trust God or others? If you've been hurt and are processing through a time of healing, ask yourself if you are trusting God. Read through the book of Psalms. You'll find many verses that will remind you of God's faithfulness. He can be trusted.

notes

DAY 21

Scripture:
"And this same God who takes care of me will supply all your needs from his glorious riches, which have been given to us in Christ Jesus" (Philippians 4:19).

Deep inside us, beyond anything we can comprehend, understand, or express, there is a need. This need presents itself differently in each person, because we are unique individuals. For some, it may be a need for security; for others, it may be a need for acceptance or affirmation.

Regardless of how these needs manifest in our lives, they all exist for the same reason. We need to feel loved. We need to be accepted. We need to feel worthy.

The power of this deep human need is probably one of the most compelling forces on this earth. I know I've let it control my life on more than one occasion. It has the potential to remove all sense of responsibility, of commitment, of reality. It releases your mind into a fantasyland where you feel completely fulfilled because you're valued.

Satan knows we're vulnerable in this area, and he'll throw anything in our paths to tempt us. He will nudge us to feel worthless. He'll fuel a cycle of negative thoughts in our mind. And then he'll present us with opportunities to receive that validation elsewhere, even though we can and should only find it in Christ. Only He can meet all our needs.

Reflect:
If we don't acknowledge our neediness when we're burned out, our lack of identity and perceived lack of value can present itself in emotional affairs, physical affairs, or codependency. We must do everything we can to protect our relational integrity. List specifically what you are doing to protect your relational integrity.

notes

DAY 22

Scripture:
"Do you have the gift of helping others? Do it with all the strength and energy that God supplies. . . . Dear friends, don't be surprised at the fiery trials you are going through, as if something strange were happening to you. Instead, be very glad —for these trials make you partners with Christ in his suffering, so that you will have the wonderful joy of seeing his glory when it is revealed to the world (1 Peter 4:11b–13).

"Do it with all the strength and energy that God supplies." This verse, and those surrounding it, struck me with new weight. Whatever gifts we have, including the gift of helping and ministering, we must use without hesitation or laziness. It is God who gives those gifts to us, and it is He who will equip us with the strength to complete what He calls us to. When we begin walking in our own strength, even if we are doing good work, we will feel far from our Savior.

The sufferings Paul writes of in this letter, and in many of the epistles, are to encourage new Christians who are persecuted in their faith. His message can also build us up as we face sufferings when we help others. Discouragement, even depression, can haunt us and take away our energy: spiritual, physical, and emotional.

Reflect:
Paul reminds us that even though we will face suffering as we allow God to work through us, we also get "the wonderful joy of seeing his glory when it is revealed to the world." Have you ever been discouraged, but on seeing a glimpse of God's work, you were filled with almost instant joy?

There's a big difference between being discouraged and having clinical depression. If you find yourself feeling discouraged and unmotivated for more than a couple of weeks and you're not sure why, talk to a pastor, counselor, or doctor to explore your symptoms and make a plan to help you get healthy.

notes

DAY 23

Scripture:
"For all who have entered into God's rest have rested from their labors, just as God did after creating the world. So let us do our best to enter that rest. But if we disobey God, as the people of Israel did, we will fall" (Hebrews 4:10-11).

Remember being a kid and hating naps? Or maybe you have children and you know how hard it is to get them to go to bed. Whenever I see children putting up a fight about naps, I think to myself, "You don't know how good you have it! You GET to sleep, and nobody expects you to do anything different!"

I've suffered from a debilitating form of insomnia since I was 14. I've been on every sleeping pill (most have the opposite effect and get me wired up) and have finally found a good combination of herbal supplements and a mild sedative, plus a very strict evening routine. Finally finding a routine and sticking to it has helped me develop a healthy sleeping rhythm.

Some people say they're night owls, others say they're early birds. I'll leave my personal beliefs about this out, but I have seen the benefits of an "early to bed; early to rise" schedule.

What's important is that you and I are getting enough rest. Our physical health depends on it. Our bodies heal with rest. Our minds reboot with sleep. Even our emotional health benefits from the subconscious processing that occurs when we sleep.

Reflect:
Do you have problems with sleep or insomnia? Could you take some time as you work through this devotional to try a new routine? Leaving bright lights (TVs, tablets, cell phones) out of the bedroom and having an unlit alarm clock helps our bodies realize that it's dark and time to sleep. Avoiding caffeine after certain hours, as well as eating late, also can contribute to a good night's rest. Try to keep a consistent bedtime routine for the next few weeks and see if you notice your mind, body, and spirit feeling better.

notes

DAY 24

Prayer days in this devotional (every sixth day) are designed to help you listen to and converse with God on anything (a scripture, an issue at hand, a praise). Maybe use the prayer section every day to supplement your daily prayers. The following structure is created to help you navigate and focus. If it doesn't fit your needs specifically, simply modify it as you need to. This isn't about getting it right; it's about communing with your Abba, Father.

• Choose a scripture that is familiar to you or that has spoken to you recently. If none comes to mind, consider one in this devotional or ask God to guide you one.

• While resting in a quiet place with no distractions, read and recite this scripture out loud several times, paying special attention to each and every word.

• Take a few moments to quiet your heart and mind. Simply sit in the presence of God, listening. If you don't hear anything or if your mind wanders, it's okay. If you don't "feel" anything, that doesn't mean God isn't saying anything. Just try to bring your attention back and focus on the idea or Bible verse at hand.

• After some time listening and sitting before God, make a list, mentally or maybe written, of things you are thankful for this week. Share them with Him and praise Him for the work He's doing.

• Confess any sins to Him, asking Him to reveal areas in your life where you can rely more fully on Him.

• Write down anything, no matter how seemingly small, that comes to mind after you spend time with Him today.

notes

DAY 25

Scripture:
"And so, dear brothers and sisters, I plead with you to give your bodies to God because of all he has done for you. Let them be a living and holy sacrifice—the kind he will find acceptable. This is truly the way to worship him" (Romans 12:1).

Ministry requires sacrifice. The Christian life requires sacrifice. But when Jesus died on the cross, the need for Old Testament sacrifices died with him. Jesus is and was and always will be the ultimate sacrifice.

God has always wanted sacrifices that come from humble hearts that look to him in faith, hearts infused with the new life of the Holy Spirit, hearts transformed to live and love like Jesus. He does not want the sacrifices of those who do not live holy and pleasing lives. The Old Testament prophets make it clear that God would prefer that people not worship him at all than that they worship him while living a lifestyle of injustice (see Isaiah 1:1–17; Amos 5:21– 24; Malachi 1:10–11).

Realize there's a difference between what you feel you must sacrifice and what God actually requires. The only sacrifice He requires is you. You sacrifice yourself to Him. We are living sacrifices, holy and pleasing to God. Offering ourselves up to Him is our act of worship. That is the only sacrifice He requires.
Live and rest fully and abundantly in that promise. His mercy and His grace will take care of the rest.

Reflect:
How can you rest in the fact that the only sacrifice God requires is of you? Not what you do but you? Ask Him to show you how small acts of faithfulness delight Him.

notes

DAY 26

Scripture:
"The thief comes only to steal and kill and destroy; I have come that they may have life, and have it to the full" (John 10:10, NIV).

The one objective the enemy has is to steal, kill, and destroy you. You may have heard somebody say, "If you're doing really good work for the Lord, Satan's going to try to stop you," or, "When you're really a threat to the devil, that's when he'll attack the hardest."

I don't think there is an "if" or a "when" about it. Satan is out to destroy you no matter what! And if Satan can put things in your path to trip you up and take others down with you, I'm sure there's no better way he'd rather spend his time. He's going to ask himself how he can kill as many birds with one stone as possible. When the death and destruction of Christ-followers is the main goal, the enemy is going to think strategically.

But that's the amazing thing about grace. Regardless of how we struggle or how we fall, regardless of how many people are affected by our actions, God is a God of healing. God is a God of restoration and life.

Reflect:
Satan loves to steal and destroy what God has intended for good. He wants us to kill our ministry, our passion, and our hope so we become useless. Through Christ, we're made complete. It's time to truly realize that and begin to claim back what is rightfully ours.

notes

DAY 27

Scripture:
"By this all people will know that you are my disciples, if you have love for one another" (John 13:35, ESV).

I think that everyone feels needs to belong. Do you? Are you caught fighting the contradiction of needing others, being needed, and wanting to be on your own? Does fear keep you from reaching out to others? Do you want to know how to strengthen the community where you live and love?

John 13:35 is just one of many scriptures that helps push us forward in our quest of desiring genuine relationships and community.

We will not find perfect community on this planet. The only perfect union that exists is between God the Father, Jesus Christ the Son, and the Holy Spirit. Until we continue on into our eternal lives after we pass from this earth, we will never encounter the unadulterated and pure communion in the way it was meant to be experienced before the fall in Eden.

However, we're not called to be perfect. We're urged to seek the Kingdom and live holy lives fully dependent on God and in relationship with others. It is first in this dependence on God, and then in our interdependence with other believers as the Spirit unites us, where we can experience a truly joyful and abundant community here on earth as it is in heaven.

Reflect:
Sadly, many people in the church have been abused or taken advantage of when they have submitted themselves to other people's authority. Because of these painful experiences, the idea of surrendering or submitting to others in relationships is frightening and can be met with a tremendous amount of resistance. Do you find yourself hesitant when it comes to the idea of inviting another person in to your life in such an intimate and vulnerable way?

notes

DAY 28

Scripture:
"And now, dear brothers and sisters, one final thing. Fix your thoughts on what is true, and honorable, and right, and pure, and lovely, and admirable. Think about things that are excellent and worthy of praise" (Philippians 4:8).

Sometimes our hearts just get weary. When all of what we're doing comes piling up over time, the word "stress" is an understatement. And without perspective or correction, our feelings of discouragement can go one of two ways: anger or apathy.

Life seems to go by and nobody seems to notice or care. We are hurt and maybe have even expressed that hurt with no response. Slowly, our need for justice creeps in, and we focus on our pain. The pain is so loud that we can't see the good things in our life.

Or, instead of our pain snowballing into anger, we choose to feel nothing. Sometimes, we think feeling nothing is a better option than feeling angry or hurt. In our apathy, we don't feel pain, but we also don't feel joy.

Reflect:
Emotions move us powerfully. Often, we make decisions based on how we feel. God doesn't want us to live with unhealthy emotions, and He also doesn't want us to live with a lack of them. God's desire is for us to find joy in spite of our circumstances.

When faced with seasons of stress or pain, do you tend to allow your emotions to build up into anger? Or do you numb them into apathy? When you're faced with emotional overload (or when you begin to feel emotionless), list a few things you're grateful for in your life or ways you've seen God move. What are some things that are true, honorable, right, pure, lovely, and admirable?

notes

DAY 29

Scripture:
"Are any among you sick? They should call for the elders of the church and have them pray over them, anointing them with oil in the name of the Lord" (James 5:14).

Eating healthy, sleeping enough, and exercising are all great ways we become and stay physically healthy. But physical health isn't just a compartment separated from the rest of our well being. James 5:14 engages all areas into our physical health.

If we are sick, we should call for the elders of the church. We must reach out and confess that we are hurting or that we are physically sick. This takes humility (emotional health) and inviting others into our weakness (relational health) so they may pray over us, and so we can exercise our faith together (spiritual health).

Reflect:
Is there an area in your physical health that is suffering? Have you shared this with another person? If not, what are some reasons that you haven't? Now that you have some tools and ideas to take steps in this area in your life, who can you bring along?

If you're struggling with anything in relation to your physical health, write those things here:

Who can you ask into your life to pray with you over these issues?

notes

DAY 30

Prayer days in this devotional (every sixth day) are designed to help you listen to and converse with God on anything (a scripture, an issue at hand, a praise). Maybe use the prayer section every day to supplement your daily prayers. The following structure is created to help you navigate and focus. If it doesn't fit your needs specifically, simply modify it as you need to. This isn't about getting it right; it's about communing with your Abba, Father.

• Choose a scripture that is familiar to you or that has spoken to you recently. If none comes to mind, consider one in this devotional or ask God to guide you one.

• While resting in a quiet place with no distractions, read and recite this scripture out loud several times, paying special attention to each and every word.

• Take a few moments to quiet your heart and mind. Simply sit in the presence of God, listening. If you don't hear anything or if your mind wanders, it's okay. If you don't "feel" anything, that doesn't mean God isn't saying anything. Just try to bring your attention back and focus on the idea or Bible verse at hand.

• After some time listening and sitting before God, make a list, mentally or maybe written, of things you are thankful for this week. Share them with Him and praise Him for the work He's doing.

• Confess any sins to Him, asking Him to reveal areas in your life where you can rely more fully on Him.

• Write down anything, no matter how seemingly small, that comes to mind after you spend time with Him today.

notes

MORE RESOURCES

For more resources on preventing or

recovering from church burnout, visit

http://www.churchburnout.com

Mad Church Disease: Healing from Church Burnout

(eBook, Paperback, Audio)

Healing from Church Burnout Study Guide

Burnout Assessment Worksheet

Healing from Church Burnout Health Plan Individual

Coaching Opportunities

Church Team and Staff Assessment and Workshops

OTHER BOOKS

By Anne Marie Miller

Permission to Speak Freely:

Essays and Art on Fear Confession and Grace

(August 2010)

Interlude: Poetry and Stories

(May 2012)

Mad Church Disease: Healing from Church Burnout

(February 2014)

Lean on Me: Finding Intentional, Vulnerable and

Consistent Community

(October 2014)

AnneMarieMiller.com

Twitter • Facebook • Instagram

@GirlNamedAnne